Federal Telework: Office of Personnel Management's 2012 Telework Report Shows Opportunities for Improvement

GAO

U.S. GOVERNMENT ACCOUNTABILITY OFFICE

441 G St. N.W.
Washington, DC 20548

June 28, 2013

The Honorable Thomas R. Carper
Chairman
The Honorable Tom Coburn
Ranking Member
Committee on Homeland Security
    and Governmental Affairs
United States Senate

The Honorable Darrell Issa
Chairman
The Honorable Elijah E. Cummings
Ranking Member
Committee on Oversight
    and Government Reform
House of Representatives

Subject: *Federal Telework: Office of Personnel Management's 2012 Telework Report Shows Opportunities for Improvement*

The Telework Enhancement Act of 2010[1] requires the Office of Personnel Management (OPM) to submit an annual report to Congress addressing the telework program of each executive agency. The act also required us to review OPM's first report and submit a report to Congress on the progress each executive agency has made towards the goals established under the act.[2] We fulfilled the mandate with a briefing to staff from both committees on our preliminary findings during the first week of May 2013. This report transmits the final briefing slides and includes recommendations we are making to the Acting Director of OPM. See enclosure I for the briefing slides.

We assessed the extent to which OPM's *2012 Status of Telework in the Federal Government: Report to the Congress* reported and assessed progress of federal executive agencies' telework participation and outcomes, including societal impacts and cost savings. Separately, we also gathered additional information regarding challenges smaller agencies may have encountered in implementing telework programs.

---

[1]Pub. L. No. 111-292, 124 Stat. 3165 (Dec. 9, 2010), codified primarily at chapter 65 of title 5, United States Code.

[2]The original date for the GAO mandate was January 3, 2013. Congressional staff agreed to postpone this and we agreed a briefing in May 2013 would suit their needs followed by issuing this report.

To conduct this work, we

- reviewed OPM's reporting requirements in the Telework Enhancement Act of 2010;[3] and reviewed OPM's 2012 report to Congress;

- analyzed selected responses from the 87 agencies that responded to OPM's 2011 data call, evaluated how Federal Employee Viewpoint Survey (FEVS) data were used, and examined how OPM conducted and reported findings from its focus groups. We found the data from both sources sufficiently reliable for assessing OPM's 2012 Status of Telework report and reporting select findings from both of these sources;

- reviewed related documentation, including FEVS questions pertaining to telework, and compared them to how OPM presented the information in its report;

- interviewed OPM officials responsible for overseeing the report; and

- held a discussion group with a random sample of 10 members of the Small Agency Human Resources Council who are knowledgeable of telework to discuss what challenges, if any, small agencies may face in implementing telework programs. The insights gained from the discussions were not generalizable to all small agencies.

We conducted this performance audit from June 2012 to May 2013 in accordance with generally accepted government auditing standards. Those standards require that we plan and perform the audit to obtain sufficient, appropriate evidence to provide a reasonable basis for our findings and conclusions based on our audit objectives. We believe that the evidence obtained provides a reasonable basis for our findings and conclusions based on our audit objectives.

In summary,

- OPM partially reported on two of the act's seven reporting requirements, but did not report agency information for the five remaining requirements. This was because insufficient time had elapsed for all requirements of the act to be fully implemented and because agencies appeared to face challenges in measuring outcomes for some nonparticipation goals, according to OPM.

- OPM recognizes weaknesses in agency sources for telework participation and frequency data, but has not taken adequate steps to establish a completion date by which agencies will produce reliable data from employee time and attendance tracking systems, which OPM defines as the most reliable tracking method.

- The small agency discussion group reported telework challenges similar to those expressed by officials from larger agencies. These challenges include management resistance and technology limitations. In addition, officials from small agencies expressed particular concerns about office impacts when a teleworking employee has no backup in the workplace and about the limited funding available for information technology to support telework.

---

[3]As part of our review, we assessed whether OPM reported on each reporting requirement using a scale of "reported," "partially reported," and "not reported." We used our professional judgment to develop each assessment.

We are making the following recommendations to the Acting Director of OPM:

1. In preparation for the 2014 telework report, OPM should provide goal setting assistance for agencies not yet able to report telework goals, including agencies which intend to establish nonparticipation goals but are not yet able to report on these goals. OPM should request in its data call that each of these agencies report by what year the agency will be able to report its goals, including each agency's timetable for complete reporting and the status of action steps and milestones they established to gauge progress.

2. OPM should include in its 2014 report to Congress the amount of cost savings resulting from the impacts of telework each agency may have identified, and the method the agency used to assess or verify the savings.

3. To improve the reliability of data collection, OPM should work with the Chief Human Capital Officers (CHCO) Council and its leadership to develop documented agreements and a timetable to complete an automated tracking system or other reliable data gathering method that can be validated by OPM.

Agency Comments and Our Evaluation

We provided a draft of this report to the Acting Director of OPM on May 31, 2013, and received the agency's written comments on June 19, 2013. The comments are reprinted in enclosure II. In summary, OPM partially concurred with our first recommendation, concurred with our second recommendation, and stated it has completed our third recommendation.

OPM partially concurred with our first recommendation that it should provide agencies with goal setting assistance and request additional information from agencies not yet able to report telework goals regarding their plans and timetable for complete reporting. OPM stated the recommendation should be limited only to agency participation goals, as the act does not require agencies to identify nonparticipation goals. OPM noted it will continue to consult with agencies to address agency competency gaps in strategic goal setting, measurement, and data collection. The act requires OPM to assist each agency in establishing appropriate qualitative and quantitative measures and teleworking goals. The act does not limit this assistance to participation goals. While agencies are not mandated to establish specified nonparticipation goals, to the extent they intend to do so, OPM should provide assistance. In addition, OPM will rely on input from the agencies to meet its reporting requirement of assessments of agency progress in meeting agency participation rate goals and, for agencies which choose to establish nonparticipation goals, an assessment of the progress made in meeting such goals. Any assessment of progress would necessarily include an identification of the goal itself. We revised our recommendation to underscore the voluntary nature of agency nonparticipation goals.

OPM concurred with our second recommendation to include the amount of cost savings that agencies have identified resulting from the impact of telework in its 2014 report. OPM stated that the act does not require agencies to report cost savings, which we acknowledged by limiting the scope of the recommendation to agencies which "may have identified" cost savings. OPM will ask agencies to identify the amount of cost savings resulting from telework and the methodology the agency used to assess or verify the savings and report the results in its 2014 annual report.

OPM stated that it has completed our third recommendation to improve the reliability of its data collection. OPM stated that during the summer of 2012 payroll providers agreed to documented standards for automated data collection of telework participation. OPM stated that it is working closely with payroll providers to complete the automation project in time for the 2015 telework status report. Further, it stated that the CHCO Council has been briefed and is aware of the effort. However, OPM has yet to establish documented agreements with the CHCO Council that would assure OPM that it will obtain the reliable agency data necessary to establish an automated tracking system. While OPM has established a date for reporting reliable data, it has not included dates for completing key activities it has identified, such as comparing telework participation, frequency, and eligibility data collected through its annual agency telework data call, with data collected through automated payroll systems.

Documented agreements between OPM and the CHCO Council would formally commit agencies to complete the necessary actions to adopt automated systems or other acceptable reliable data gathering methods. A completed timetable is needed because it could specify the milestones, required sub-tasks to be completed and their dates. Until OPM demonstrates it has specified the necessary steps to develop documented agreements with the CHCO Council and its leadership and identified all of the required sub-tasks to complete the development of an automated tracking system or other reliable data gathering method, OPM cannot be confident that it will be in a position to report reliable data in 2015 as it intends.

In addition to officials at both committees, we are sending copies of this report to other interested congressional committees, officials at OPM, the Executive Director of the CHCO Council, and the small agency officials who participated in our discussion group. In addition, the report will be available at no charge on the GAO website at http://www.gao.gov.

Should you and your office have questions or matters discussed in this report, please contact me at (202) 512-6806 or at jonesy@gao.gov. Contact points for our Offices of Congressional Relations and Public Affairs may be found on the last page of our report. GAO staff who made key contributions to this reported are listed in enclosure III.

Yvonne D. Jones, Director
Strategic Issues

Final Briefing Slides Prepared for the Senate Committee on Homeland Security and Governmental Affairs and House of Representatives Committee on Oversight and Government Reform

GAO's Review of OPM's 2012 Telework Report

Prepared for the Senate Committee on Homeland Security and Governmental Affairs and House of Representatives Committee on Oversight and Government Reform

May 3, 2013

Page 1

Overview

- Objectives, Scope, and Methodology

- Results in Brief

- Background

- Findings

- Conclusions

- Recommendations for Executive Action

Page 2

Objectives

In response to a mandate in the Telework Enhancement Act of 2010, we reviewed the first required Office of Personnel Management (OPM) report to Congress on the telework programs of each executive agency. We assessed the extent to which OPM's *2012 Status of Telework in the Federal Government: Report to the Congress* reported and assessed progress of federal executive agencies' telework participation and outcomes, including societal impacts and cost savings.

Separately, we also gathered additional information regarding challenges smaller agencies may have encountered in implementing telework programs.

Page 3

Scope and Methodology

To conduct this work, we:

- reviewed OPM's reporting requirements in the Telework Enhancement Act of 2010 and reviewed OPM's 2012 report to Congress;

- analyzed selected responses from the 87 agencies that responded to OPM's 2011 data call, evaluated how Federal Employee Viewpoint Survey (FEVS) data were used, and examined how OPM conducted and reported findings from its focus groups;

- reviewed related documentation, including FEVS questions pertaining to telework, and compared them to how OPM presented the information in its report;

- interviewed OPM officials responsible for overseeing the report; and

- held a discussion group with a random sample of 10 members of the Small Agency Human Resources Council who are knowledgeable of telework to discuss what challenges, if any, small agencies may face in implementing telework programs. The insights gained from the discussions were not generalizable to all small agencies.

Page 4

Generally Accepted Government Auditing Standards

We conducted this performance audit from June 2012 to May 2013 in accordance with generally accepted government auditing standards. Those standards require that we plan and perform the audit to obtain sufficient, appropriate evidence to provide a reasonable basis for our findings and conclusions based on our audit objectives. We believe that the evidence obtained provides a reasonable basis for our findings and conclusions based on our audit objectives.

Page 5

Results in Brief

- OPM partially reported on two of the act's seven reporting requirements, but did not report agency information for the five remaining requirements. This was because insufficient time had elapsed for all requirements of the act to be fully implemented and because agencies appeared to face challenges in measuring outcomes for some nonparticipation goals, according to OPM.

- OPM recognizes weaknesses in agency sources for telework participation and frequency data, but has not taken adequate steps to establish a completion date by which agencies will produce reliable data from employee time and attendance (T&A) tracking systems, which OPM defines as the most reliable tracking method.

- The small agency discussion group reported telework challenges similar to those expressed by officials from larger agencies. These challenges include management resistance and technology limitations. In addition, officials from small agencies expressed particular concerns about office impacts when a teleworking employee has no backup in the workplace and about the limited funding available for information technology to support telework.

Page 6

Background

- Telework offers various flexibilities for both employers and employees, including the capacity to continue operations during emergency events, as well as benefits to society, such as decreased energy use and pollution.

- The Telework Enhancement Act of 2010[1] made a large step forward in transforming the approach to telework by establishing a framework of requirements for executive agencies to meet in implementing telework. These requirements include notifying all employees of their eligibility to telework and establishing agency telework participation goals for the measurement and reporting of results.

[1] Pub. L. No. 111-292, 124 Stat. 3165 (Dec. 9, 2010).

Page 7

Background

The act assigns OPM major leadership responsibilities. Responsibilities include:

- Provide policy and policy guidance for telework in areas such as agency closure and performance management.

- Assist each agency in establishing appropriate qualitative and quantitative measures and teleworking goals.

- Submit an annual report, in consultation with the Chief Human Capital Officers (CHCO) Council, to Congress addressing the telework programs of each executive agency. The act requires OPM to report on seven elements, such as each agency's degree of telework participation and an assessment of each agency's progress in meeting its telework goals.

- Include in the annual telework report relevant information from reports prepared by agency CHCOs, in consultation with agency telework managing officers (TMOs), that were submitted to the Chair and Vice Chair of the CHCO Council on agency management efforts to promote telework.

- Identify best practices and recommendations for the federal government and review the outcomes associated with an increase in telework, including effects on energy consumption, job creation and availability, urban transportation patterns, and the ability to anticipate the dispersal of work during periods of emergency.

Page 8

Background

OPM's 2012 report to Congress is based primarily on three data sources:

- 2011 OPM Telework Data Call

    The data call allows OPM to systematically collect agency telework data, such as participation levels and frequency. Agencies are required to participate in the data call in order for OPM to fulfill its reporting obligation under the act.

- 2011 FEVS selected questions that pertain to telework

    FEVS is designed to provide insights into the challenges agency leaders face in ensuring the federal government has an effective civilian workforce.

    We found the data from both sources sufficiently reliable for assessing OPM's 2012 Status of Telework report and reporting select findings from both of these sources.

- Focus groups with TMOs and telework coordinators

    Twenty agencies were represented in the focus groups.

Page 9

OPM Has Partially Reported on 2 of the Act's 7 Reporting Requirements

Table 1: Summary of Extent OPM Reported on the Requirements of the Telework Enhancement Act of 2010

OPM reporting requirements	Extent reported
1) Participation and frequency of eligible employees	Partially reported
2) Method for gathering telework data in each agency	Not reported
3) If the total number of employees teleworking is 10 percent higher or lower than the previous year in any agency, the reasons for the variation	Not reported
4) Agency goal for participation by frequency category	Not reported
5) Whether agencies met goals and, if not, what actions are being taken to maximize telework opportunities	Not reported
6) Assessment of progress for meeting participation goals and other goals	Not reported
7) Best practices in agency telework programs	Partially reported

Source: GAO analysis of OPM's *2012 Status of Telework in the Federal Government: Report to the Congress.* Page 10

OPM Did Not Collect and Report Participation Goals in the Form Required by the Act

- The act requires OPM to report agency goals for increasing participation as a percentage of eligible employees teleworking and their frequency. OPM reported that it did not do so because some agencies were not ready or able to set participation goals. Agencies were not required to establish participation and frequency goals prior to the act.

- OPM reported that of the agencies responding to the data call, 41 (47 percent) had established numeric participation goals. These agency participation goals were either a percentage or a number of employees participating in telework. Twenty-seven agencies (31 percent) did not report a participation goal. In addition, 19 agencies (22 percent) declined to give a numeric goal, but gave a descriptive goal.

- In March 2013, OPM advised us it had collected the status of agency telework participation goals in late fall of 2012 and would report on the status in its 2013 report to Congress. Further, OPM officials stated that agencies will be asked to establish goals in the form required by the act to be reported in OPM's 2014 report to Congress.

Page 11

OPM Did Not Report Whether Each Agency Met Its Participation Goals

- OPM did not report whether each agency met its participation goals because these goals had not yet been established. This report set a baseline for future reporting of whether agencies had met its goals.

- OPM officials told us that OPM's 2013 telework report to Congress will

  - report whether participation goals were met and, if not, what actions the agency was taking to maximize telework in the next reporting period.

  - rely on agency self-assessments of progress, provided to OPM through its data call process.

Page 12

OPM Did Not Report Assessments of Progress Meeting Other Agency Telework-Related Goals

- The act also requires an assessment of each agency's progress in meeting other goals the agency may have established, such as the impact of telework on recruitment and retention and energy use. As a result of the act, OPM revised the 2011 data call to collect agency information about other telework-related goals. As this had not been collected before, there was no baseline to use to report progress.

- OPM reported how many agencies have set nonparticipation goals and the number of agencies reporting they had achieved cost savings in various categories, such as rent and utilities. OPM reported, for example, 53 agencies (66 percent) that provided data about outcome goals stated they had established goals for recruitment, 52 agencies (65 percent) for retention, and 26 agencies (33 percent) for reduced energy use. Also, cost savings estimates are still in the planning stages for 29 agencies and 15 agencies reported they do not track or did not realize cost savings. OPM did not report each agency's specific agency goal in the various categories, if the agency had established one.

- OPM reported that it appears agencies are facing challenges when measuring goal outcomes related to reducing commuter miles, energy use, and agency real estate costs and improved employee performance. OPM suggested the lack of readily available data and the difficulty of measuring these outcomes may be dissuading agencies from focusing attention on other goals.

Page 13

OPM Noted Limitations to Its 2012 Report, but Anticipates Improvements to Future Reports

- The 2012 report established a new baseline for future reporting periods, but:
  - Participation and frequency numbers in the 2012 report may under-report telework activity because many agencies do not have the systems capacity to collect all requested data.
  - OPM reported it is working with payroll providers and agencies to implement a standardized government-wide data collection system.

Page 14

OPM Noted Limitations to Its 2012 Report, but Anticipates Improvements to Future Reports

- The act makes it mandatory for all teleworkers to have entered into a written telework agreement with an agency manager.

- Some agencies had not yet developed databases to track the number of signed telework agreements. As a result, the government-wide totals for number of agreements and number of teleworkers do not match, with more employees teleworking than employees with telework agreements. OPM states this is a limitation in data collection rather than a failure to ensure signed agreements.

Page 15

Other Limitations—Management Efforts to Promote Telework Were Not Reviewed

- Agency telework reports of management efforts to promote telework were not reviewed by the CHCO Council leadership for relevant information to report to Congress.
  - The act requires relevant information from agencies' annual telework reports to be included in OPM's annual report to Congress.
  - OPM stated it did not request agency reports on management efforts to promote telework due to an unclear understanding of roles and responsibilities within OPM.
  - OPM added a question to the data call for the 2013 report asking agencies to address how their management promotes telework.

Page 16

Other Limitations—No Data Collected on the Amount of Cost Savings

- OPM did not collect data on the amount of cost savings resulting from telework.
  - In the 2011 data call, about one-third of agencies (28 agencies) reported achieving cost savings from telework in areas such as reduced rent or office space and transportation subsidies, but OPM did not request specific amounts. Three agencies chose to report a specific estimated amount.
  - OPM officials stated they continue to consult with agencies to help them set standards and develop assessment tools. In addition, OPM was exploring possible data sources to help agencies establish and assess progress on some of the more difficult to measure goals (e.g., commuting, energy savings).

Page 17

OPM's Report Updates Efforts to Improve Data Collection

- OPM reported many agencies do not have the systems capacity to collect all requested data, which has consequences for data quality standards, including reliability.

- In its 2012 report, OPM reported it has worked closely with payroll providers and agencies to develop a government-wide set of standards for data collection. It has also established a statement of work to automate the collection of government-wide telework data, which includes the initial period, milestones, and time frames for comparing agency data collected through automated systems with data collected through prior methods.

- However, no completion date for the project has been established and OPM reports that a timetable for completion is not entirely under its control. For example, some agencies do not yet have automated T&A systems and may not have funding available to meet the completion date OPM may request.

- OPM's statement of work states that ideally, data collected through the automated system would be used for the 2015 report to Congress.

Page 18

Comparison of Large and Small Agency Views of Telework Challenges

Telework representatives from both large and small agencies identified similar challenges.[2]

- Eighty percent of the agencies (16 agencies) in OPM's focus groups had more than 1,700 employees. Challenges reported by OPM in its focus groups included:
  - manager resistance;
  - technology related challenges;
  - equity with which telework has been made available to employees;
  - performance management; and
  - access to senior leadership.

- Eighty percent of the agencies (8 agencies) in our discussion group had fewer than 1,700 employees. Challenges reported by discussion group participants included:
  - management resistance;
  - technology related challenges;
  - office coverage; and
  - budget and funding.

[2] We defined an agency's size based on whether OPM's report indicated the agency had 1,700 employees.

Page 19

Scope and Methodology for Obtaining Additional Small Agency Insights

We held a group discussion with officials from small agencies regarding challenges faced in implementing telework programs in their agencies.

- For the purposes of our analysis, we identified small agencies as members of the Small Agency Human Resources Council, which generally have 500 or fewer employees.
- Representatives from 10 agencies, which had provided data for the 2012 OPM report, were randomly selected to participate in a 90-minute discussion.

Table 2: Agencies Participating in GAO's Small Agency Discussion Group

Commodity Futures Trading Commission	National Labor Relations Board
Court Services and Offender Supervision Agency	Overseas Private Investment Corporation
Institute of Museum and Library Services	Surface Transportation Board
Merit Systems Protection Board	U.S. Agency for International Development
National Credit Union Administration	U.S. International Trade Commission

Source: GAO.

Page 20

Small Agency Challenges

Management Resistance

A number of agency officials said their agency needs to change its perspective concerning telework. One element that needs to change is different expectations for teleworkers and non-teleworkers.

- An official said some less experienced managers require a written report from teleworkers summarizing what they accomplished while teleworking.
- Officials at two agencies stated employees at their agency cannot both telework and have an alternative work schedule.
- One official stated that management resistance due to an "old school" management style of face-to-face interaction is a current challenge.

Information Technology

A number of agency officials said the cost of implementing information technology solutions to increase telework was a challenge.

- For example, an official said that during Hurricane Sandy the agency did not have sufficient software licenses to accommodate all teleworking employees. The official said his agency has about double the number of licenses it needs to support the normal teleworking load, but it is not sufficient for widespread teleworking, and licenses are very costly.

Page 21

Small Agency Challenges

Office Coverage

Agency officials cited challenges covering positions where one individual serves as the only agency official for that responsibility.

- Several agency officials indicated that they believed this was unique to being at a small agency since larger agencies would likely have multiple individuals to cover a function. They felt that larger agencies could better cover unexpected on-site needs by having other employees on-site with the required knowledge and skills.

- To address the issue of office coverage, an official said his agency requires a "buddy system" for teleworkers so there are backup staff in the office to meet unexpected on-site needs.

Budget and Funding

Agency officials felt that small agencies have particular challenges as the investment in technology to support telework benefits fewer employees than in large agencies, so funding may be a lesser priority.

Page 22

Conclusions

The requirements of the act put in place the elements of a new system of accountability that will enable improved oversight of agency implementation of telework programs. However, it remains uncertain when full compliance with the act's reporting requirements will be achieved.

OPM's 2012 report states that many agencies do not have the systems capacity to collect the participation and frequency data required by the act and the timeline to complete a government-wide automated system has not been established. Without a timetable for completion and agreement of stakeholders affected by this strategy, there is no assurance OPM's efforts will achieve the telework data collection system it needs or that an alternative collection and reporting strategy will be developed.

Page 23

Conclusions

Identifying agencies' goals, such as the impact of telework on reducing agency energy use, commuter miles, and reducing or avoiding real estate costs, is an important element of consideration in providing an assessment of agency progress in meeting such goals.

OPM has taken steps to satisfy the act's requirements and understands the significance of the act for both agencies and federal employees. The report makes clear OPM sees its role as one of consulting with agencies to assist in developing and advancing telework programs. Such assistance is especially valuable for agencies that have not yet been able to establish telework goals. OPM plans to focus on evaluation efforts and offer training in measurement, goal setting, and action planning.

Page 24

Recommendations to the Acting Director, OPM

1. In preparation for the 2014 telework report, OPM should provide goal setting assistance for agencies not yet able to report telework goals, including agencies which intend to establish nonparticipation goals but are not yet able to report on these goals. OPM should request in its data call that each of these agencies report by what year the agency will be able to report its goals, including each agency's timetable for complete reporting and the status of action steps and milestones they established to gauge progress.

2. OPM should include in its 2014 report to Congress the amount of cost savings resulting from the impacts of telework each agency may have identified, and the method the agency used to assess or verify the savings.

3. To improve the reliability of data collection, OPM should work with the CHCO Council and its leadership to develop documented agreements and a timetable to complete an automated tracking system or other reliable data gathering method that can be validated by OPM.

Page 25

GAO on the Web
Web site: http://www.gao.gov/

Congressional Relations
Katherine Siggerud, Managing Director, siggerudk@gao.gov
(202) 512-4400, U.S. Government Accountability Office
441 G Street, NW, Room 7125, Washington, DC 20548

Public Affairs
Chuck Young, Managing Director, youngc1@gao.gov
(202) 512-4800, U.S. Government Accountability Office
441 G Street, NW, Room 7149, Washington, DC 20548

Page 26

Comments from the Office of Personnel Management

UNITED STATES OFFICE OF PERSONNEL MANAGEMENT
Washington, DC 20415

Employee Services

JUN 1 9 2013

Yvonne D. Jones, Director
Strategic Issues
U.S. Government Accountability Office
441 G St, NW
Washington DC 20548

Dear Ms. Jones:

Thank you for providing a draft of the Government Accountability Office report, "GAO's Review of OPM's 2012 Telework Report" to the U.S. Office of Personnel Management (OPM). We appreciate the opportunity to provide you with comments about this report.

Responses to Recommendations

RECOMMENDATION 1:
In preparation for the 2014 telework report, for agencies not yet able to report telework goals, OPM should provide goal setting assistance and request in its data call that each of those agencies report by what year the agency will be able to report its goals, including each agency's timetable for complete reporting and the status of action steps and milestones they established to gauge progress.

MANAGEMENT RESPONSE:
Both participation and non-participation goals are discussed in the requirements for OPM's telework status report and, as written, it is unclear which telework goals are addressed in the recommendation. Under report content requirements, the Telework Enhancement Act (Act) mandates "[e]ach report submitted under this subsection shall include . . . (D) the agency goal for increasing participation to the extent practicable or necessary for the next reporting period" 5 U.S.C. § 6506(b)(2)(D), and requires an assessment of the progress each agency has made against those goals *id.* at § 6506(b)(2)(F).

Section 6506(b)(2)(F) also prescribes an assessment of the progress each agency has made in meeting "other agency goals," i.e., non-participation goals, such as the impact of telework on emergency readiness or energy use. It is significant, however, that the Act does not require agencies to *identify* goals in this area. In other words, there is no analogue to paragraph D of section 6506(b)(2), which imposes an obligation to report each agency's participation goals.

Yvonne D. Jones   Page 2

Assuming the recommendation is revised to stipulate *participation goals* only, OPM concurs with the recommendation. OPM engaged agency telework staff in extensive training in goal-setting, measurement, data collection design, program evaluation, and action planning in preparation for the 2011 data collection for the 2012 telework status report. We will continue to consult with agencies on those topics in an effort to address the continuing gap between telework coordinator agency staff competencies and the sophisticated strategic goal-setting, measurement and data collection competencies required to meet the Act's reporting requirements.

RECOMMENDATION 2:
OPM should include in its 2014 report to Congress the amount of cost savings resulting from the impacts of telework each agency may have identified, and the method the agency used to assess or verify the savings.

MANAGEMENT RESPONSE:
To begin, we note that the Act does not require agencies to report "cost savings" related to telework (although it does mention "energy use" in a list of potential impacts of telework as to which an agency might wish to establish goals). See 5 U.S.C. § 6506(b)(2)(F). While OPM did ask agencies in the 2011 data call if they have achieved costs savings from maintaining or implementing telework, that question was a legacy from earlier pre-Act administrations of the call. Many agencies lack the capacity or resources to capture data such as the reduction in energy use that is attributable to telework. Translating reduced energy use into costs savings would be even more challenging.

We appreciate and share, however, GAO's desire to showcase the efforts of any agency that has actually worked to collect cost data. And we would be willing to highlight any cost savings that agencies have achieved with telework. We concur with the spirit of the recommendation and will add two follow-up, *voluntary* questions to the next data call (results will appear in the 2014 report) for any agency that does calculate and report cost savings. The first item will ask the reporting agency to specify the amount of any cost savings resulting from telework for each identified outcome and, the second, the methodology the agency used to assess or verify the savings.

RECOMMENDATION 3:
To improve the reliability of its data collection, OPM should work with the CHCO council and its leadership to develop documented agreements and a timetable to complete an automated tracking system or other reliable data gathering method that can be validated by OPM.

Yvonne D. Jones   Page 3

MANAGEMENT RESPONSE:

OPM has completed this recommendation. As GAO is aware, payroll providers and telework managing officers/coordinators engaged in data automation planning meetings with OPM during the summer of 2012. During that time, payroll providers agreed to documented standards for automated data collection of telework participation. OPM is working closely with payroll providers to complete the automation project in time for the 2015 telework status report. The Chief Human Capital Officers (CHCO) Council has been briefed and is aware of the effort.

Please contact Ms. Janet Barnes, Director, Internal Oversight & Compliance on (202) 606-3270, should your office require additional information.

Again, thank you for providing this opportunity to update and clarify information in the draft report.

Sincerely,

Angela Bailey
Associate Director
Employee Services

GAO Contact and Staff Acknowledgements

GAO Contact

Yvonne D. Jones, (202) 512-6806 or jonesy@gao.gov

Staff Acknowledgements

In addition to the contact listed above, key contributors to this report were William Doherty, Assistant Director; Shea Bader, James Cook, Analyst-In-Charge; Jenny Chanley, Jeff DeMarco, Karin Fangman and Robert Gebhart.

Related GAO Products

Federal Telework: Program Measurement Continues to Confront Data Reliability Issues. GAO-12-519. Washington, D.C.: April 19, 2012.

Emergency Preparedness: Agencies Need Coordinated Guidance on Incorporating Telework into Emergency and Continuity Planning. GAO-11-628. Washington, D.C.: July 22, 2011.

Human Capital: Telework Programs Need Clear Goals and Reliable Data. GAO-08-261T. Washington, D.C.: November 6, 2007.

Human Capital: Greater Focus on Results in Telework Programs Needed. GAO-07-1002T. Washington, D.C.: June 12, 2007.

Agency Telework Methodologies: Departments of Commerce, Justice, State, the Small Business Administration, and the Securities and Exchange Commission. GAO-05-1055R. Washington, D.C.: September 27, 2005.

Human Capital: Key Practices to Increasing Federal Telework. GAO-04-950T. Washington, D.C.: July 8, 2004.

Human Capital: Further Guidance, Assistance, and Coordination Can Improve Federal Telework Efforts. GAO-03-679. Washington, D.C.: July 18, 2003.

(450993)

www.ingramcontent.com/pod-product-compliance
Lightning Source LLC
Chambersburg PA
CBHW081132280526
45787CB00007B/3056